$7.95

THE TOMB ROBBERS

DANIEL COHEN

illustrated with photographs and old prints

Tomb robbing is an ancient, widespread, persistent, and sometimes even honorable occupation, according to Daniel Cohen. The tomb robbers have had a great deal of influence on what we know about ancient history. That is why King Tutankhamun is better known than Ramses II. The robbers got to Ramses' tomb but left Tutankhamun's almost intact.

A thoughtful discussion of the boy king, his place in history, and his tomb sets off the author's lively investigation of tomb robbers. He explains why the pyramids failed completely to protect the royal mummies and treasure, although the elaborate designs of their interiors were intended to thwart robbers. He describes the "mummy's curse"; tells how the priests of ancient times tried to prevent robberies by

(continued on back flap)

THE
TOMB
ROBBERS

Daniel Cohen

THE
TOMB
ROBBERS

McGRAW-HILL BOOK COMPANY

NEW YORK   ST. LOUIS   SAN FRANCISCO
BOGOTÁ   DÜSSELDORF   MADRID
MEXICO   MONTREAL   NEW DELHI   PANAMA   PARIS
SÃO PAULO   SINGAPORE   TOKYO   TORONTO

PICTURE CREDITS

Griffith Institute, Ashmolean Museum: page 6
MGM, 1964: page 75
The Metropolitan Museum of Art: page 3
Movie Star News: pages 30, 43, 44, 54, 55, 73
The New York Public Library Picture Collection: pages 4, 10, 13, 16, 19, 24, 25, 29, 33, 39, 47, 51, 59, 60, 63, 66, 67
Thames and Hudson, *The Mongols*: page 72
Twentieth Century-Fox: page 9
Universal: pages 21, 41
UPI: page 68
Cohen, Daniel, *Secrets from Ancient Graves*. New York: Dodd, Mead & Company, 1968: pages 79, 84

Library of Congress Cataloging in Publication Data

Cohen, Daniel.
    The tomb robbers.

    Bibliography: p.
    Includes index.
    SUMMARY: Discusses the ancient and widespread practice of tomb robbing in Egypt and ways the Egyptians tried to protect themselves from tomb robbers.
    1. Tombs—Egypt—Juvenile literature. 2. Egypt—Antiquities—Juvenile literature. 3. Brigands and robbers—Juvenile literature.
[1. Tombs—Egypt. 2. Egypt—Antiquities. 3. Robbers and outlaws.]
I. Title.
DT62.T6C63   932   79–22760
ISBN 0–07–011566–4

123456789RABP876543210

Contents

THE
TOMB
ROBBERS

1

Why Is King Tut So Famous?

Not long ago an exhibit of objects from the tomb of King Tutankhamun toured the United States. People stood in line for hours to get tickets to see it. I was one of them.

Was the exhibit worth the wait? For me it was. The ancient Egyptians produced some of the most beautiful and elegant objects of art ever made. Besides, just being in the presence of all that gold is truly awe-inspiring.

I suspect that when most people looked at the magnificent golden funeral mask of King Tut they thought they were gazing upon the serene features of one of the great kings of the ancient world. That idea is completely wrong. As far as kings go, Tutankhamun was a nobody—a puppet ruler.

The famous boy king was manipulated by a powerful group of court officials, generals, and priests. He was made king in 1352 B.C.; he was about nine years old at the time, too young to exercise any real power. He died in 1343 B.C. at the age of about eighteen after sitting on the throne of Egypt for only nine years. Tutankhamun was very probably murdered by the ambitious men who had put him on the throne in the first place. The boy king was succeeded by an elderly court official who didn't last long, and then by a general who had no previous connection with the royal family of Egypt.

Tutankhamun's brief reign was marked by only one major event. During that time, one of the most dramatic religious revolutions in all of ancient history was ended and reversed. Tutankhamun's predecessor was Akhenaten. This king tried to change the traditional form of religion in Egypt from the worship of many gods to the worship of a single sun god called Aten.

The change was never popular with the Egyptian priesthood or with the conservative and traditional elements of Egyptian society. Akhenaten was too absorbed in his religion to rule effectively. By the time of Akhenaten's death (possibly his murder), the Egyptian Empire was in a shambles. But the Aten religion still strongly influenced those who grew up in Akhenaten's court. So when King Tut took the throne, he first had the name Tutankh*aten*. But this was quickly changed to Tutankh*amun*. Amun is the name of one of the chief gods of the old religion.

The throne name chosen by a king was an important indication of policy, and this name change was a clear signal that the religious revolution was over. Still, the anti-Aten forces were never really satisfied with King Tut. After his death they may have tried to erase his name from official records and monuments. Tutankhamun's successors certainly did nothing to memorialize his brief reign. Sixty years ago the name Tutankhamun appeared on only a few known objects.

The solid gold funeral mask of King Tutankhamun.

The powerful god Amun (left) shown with one of the queens of Egypt.

Thus, it was familiar only to a handful of scholars. Today, however, practically everybody knows the name of this obscure and historically unimportant monarch. Yet few have heard of the really great Egyptian Kings—Thutmosis, Khufu, Zoser, Seti. Even Ramses II is not well known to the general public, and he had one of the longest reigns of any king anywhere. Ramses tried to assure his own immortal fame by having his name and likeness chiseled into practically every piece of bare rock that his workmen could reach. He often tore down the monuments of earlier kings and used the stones to erect memorials to his own greater glory. It was all in vain. The ineffectual and short-lived Tutankhamun is far, far more famous than the long-lived megalomaniac Ramses.

This dramatic reversal of fortune came about in 1922

when the British archaeologist Howard Carter and his patron Lord Carnarvon discovered the nearly unplundered tomb of Tutankhamun. The key word in that sentence is *unplundered.* The tombs of almost every other known Egyptian king had already been found. And without exception, these tombs had been destroyed or thoroughly robbed, usually centuries ago. Robbers may have entered King Tut's tomb, but they didn't go very far or get very much.

All of which brings us to the subject of our book—tomb robbers. Not only have practically all the royal Egyptian tombs been plundered, nearly all the tombs of the nobles and the wealthy have been plundered as well. Nor is tomb robbing limited to Egypt. The same story has been repeated all over the world. Tomb robbing is an ancient, widespread, persistent, and sometimes even honorable occupation. The tomb robbers have had a great deal of influence on what we know about ancient history. That is why King Tut is better known than Ramses. The robbers got to Ramses's tomb but left Tutankhamun's almost intact.

Though tomb robbing has taken place all over the world, nowhere has it been as spectacular as in Egypt, probably because nowhere else in the world have there been such glorious tombs. If there is a tomb robbers' paradise, it would have to be Egypt.

Why was the tomb of Tutankhamun alone spared by the robbers? It was probably his very obscurity that saved him. When the forces of the old gods reestablished themselves in Egypt, they tried to wipe out all traces of the hated religious revolution. The chief criminal in their view was Akhenaten. But he had held power for too many years to be entirely for-

Howard Carter (left) and associate Arthur C. Mace, opening one of the doors in King Tutankhamun's tomb.

gotten. There was too much evidence of his existence. During his reign an entirely new style of art was inaugurated. The bust of Queen Nefertiti, probably the most famous single piece of Egyptian sculpture, is an outstanding example of this new style. Akhenaten built a new capital city. After his fall, the city was abandoned. In fact, it was abandoned by Tutankhamun as part of his surrender to the forces of reaction. The abandoned city turned out to be a treasure trove for archaeologists. As a result, the reign of Akhenaten is one of the most well documented in Egyptian history. Akhenaten has emerged as sort of a hero of ancient Egypt. Several modern novels and even a motion picture have been made about him. Akhenaten's own tomb may have been destroyed by his enemies, plundered by robbers, or it may yet remain undiscovered. But more of that in a later chapter.

While destroying the memory of Akhenaten was extremely difficult, the short-lived Tutankhamun was another matter. Only hints of his existence appear in the Egyptian records. There was little to destroy, even if his enemies had wished to do so.

Tutankhamun was hastily buried in a small tomb in the Valley of the Kings—a desolate and gloomy valley, which became the final resting place of many of Egypt's greatest rulers. The kings had moved their burials to the valley in order to avoid tomb robbers. With the exception of Tutankhamun, these hopes for protection from robbers were in vain. It is entirely possible that the location of King Tut's tomb, indeed the very existence of the king, had been forgotten by potential robbers. Or perhaps they didn't feel the tomb was worth the effort.

Today we marvel at the objects from Tutankhamun's tomb. But they can only be a pale reflection of the treasures that must have rested within the tombs of the really great and rich kings. Many of the objects were actually made for the tomb of someone else, a rather shadowy figure named Smenkhkare, who may have ruled briefly between the time of Akhenaten and Tutankhamun. There is ample evidence of haste and carelessness in the burial of Tutankhamun.

Shortly after the tomb was closed, robbers seem to have gotten as far as the first chamber, but no farther. It's possible that the thieves were workmen or others actually connected with the construction of the tomb. Why they stopped short of the inner chambers where the gold was stored is unknown.

Whatever the reasons, the tomb of King Tutankhamun rested relatively undisturbed until 1922. It was then that a nearly discouraged Howard Carter came upon a series of steps cut into the rock of the Valley of the Kings.

Carter had been searching for the tomb for years. He knew of Tutankhamun's existence. He knew that the king's tomb had never been located by archaeologists. Carter also thought the tomb was intact because few objects from the tomb had ever showed up on Egypt's flourishing black market in antiquities. But by 1922 the money and patience of Carter's patron, Lord Carnarvon, were running out. This was to be Carter's last season of digging in the valley.

Then, on November 6, 1922, Carter sent a wire to Carnarvon, who was in England at the time:

AT LAST WE HAVE MADE A WONDERFUL DISCOVERY IN VAL-
LEY. MAGNIFICENT TOMB WITH SEALS INTACT. RECOVERED
SAME FOR YOUR ARRIVAL. CONGRATULATIONS.

The heretic king Akhnaton was the hero of the film "The Egyptian." Here Akhnaton (far left) is making an offering to his god, Aton, who is represented by a disc of the sun with rays ending in hands. The disc is on the wall behind the king.

A small portion of what lay beyond that sealed door was put on display for the delight and astonishment of millions of Americans. There were alabaster statues, ebony tables, and of course gold in a fantastic variety of shapes and forms.

And if this is what was left, we can only begin to imagine what was lost to the tomb robbers over the centuries.

9

Two views of the preparation of an Egyptian mummy for burial. Top, an ancient Egyptian view; bottom, a nineteenth-century view.

2

Pyramids, Camouflage, and Curses

Nearly every people, ancient and modern, has taken some special care of its dead. But no people in all history ever lavished more care upon dead bodies than the ancient Egyptians.

Preservation of the body was a fundamental part of Egyptian religion, and the Egyptians were a very religious people. They believed that everyone had a soul—called a *ka*. In order for the soul to survive, the body had to be preserved in some fashion. This idea probably developed because of the peculiar climate of Egypt. In most places, if a body is buried, it will rot after a fairly short time. When it is dug up, there will be nothing recognizable left of it.

The Egyptian climate is so hot and moisture-free that a body buried in the sands may dry out and remain remarkably well preserved. If dug up some years later, the body will be shrunken and leathery but still recognizably human.

The hot, dry climate of Egypt is the real secret of the

preservation of Egyptian mummies. There has been a great deal of nonsense written about the "secrets" of Egyptian funerary techniques. While it is quite true that the Egyptians did use very elaborate methods and expensive ointments when preparing a mummy, most of the work and expense was wasted—worse than wasted. Some of the things the Egyptians did may have actually aided in the destruction of their mummies.

The mummy of King Tut is a good example. Though the tomb itself was in excellent condition, the mummy for which the entire tomb was constructed was in terrible shape. A great deal of preservative ointment had been poured on the mummy's wrappings. This had hardened into a solid black mass that fused wrappings and mummy together. As a result, the king's mummy is in far worse condition than the mummies of many of his poorer subjects who could not afford elaborate burial arrangements.

The secret of Egyptian mummification is no secret at all. The body was cut open and internal organs removed. The corpse was then thoroughly dried, and material like straw or mud was stuffed into the body cavities so that the mummy could retain a more lifelike form.

Finally, the dried body was wrapped in a hundred yards or so of linen strips. All of this was done to the accompaniment of incredibly elaborate magical spells and rites. There were special hours-long rituals for the wrapping of each finger and toe of an important person's mummy.

Preparation of some important mummies went on for seventy days before final burial or interment took place.

Egyptian religion demanded that the mummy be housed

Mummies have always fascinated people. Here is a highly romantic, and highly inaccurate, nineteenth-century picture of a mummy being dragged around an Egyptian feast.

in the most elaborate tomb, or "house of eternity," that the dead man could afford and that he be buried with much of his own household treasure so he could use it again in the next world. These two ideas assured the development and continuing prosperity of countless generations of tomb robbers in Egypt.

When we think of Egyptian tombs, we immediately think of the pyramids, as indeed we should. The original pyramids were built over four thousand years ago. They were the first large free-standing stone constructions ever built. Though somewhat battered by time, they still stand today, and they still are enormously impressive. The pyramids are so huge and so solidly built that they may well last another four thousand years. They will certainly be around long, long after the Empire State Building, the Sears Tower, and all the other grandiose modern constructions have crumbled to rubble and been forgotten.

The pyramids are such marvelous structures that for centuries some people have insisted that the ancient Egyptians could not have built them. Speculations as to who might have "really" built the pyramids have ranged from the biblical Noah to people from outer space. But professional archaeologists scoff at all such suggestions. They insist that the Egyptians themselves could and did build the pyramids. But it wasn't easy. Building the large pyramids took the labor of thousands over a period of many years.

What was it all for? As far as we have been able to determine, the pyramids were built as tombs for the kings of Egypt. It's hard to imagine that any people would have spent so much time and effort just to build a tomb for a king, no matter how powerful that king was. But the king of Egypt was not quite like the kings of most other nations. He was not only a ruler; he was thought of as a god. (The word *pharaoh*, by the way, means "great house," and it is the way the king of Egypt is often referred to in the Bible.)

So the king's tomb was not just a tomb. In a sense it was a religious monument. The gigantic structure was supposed to express the power and glory of the god-king of Egypt. It was more like a cathedral than a tomb.

In practical terms, however, the pyramids were tombs. The king's mummy was placed in a chamber inside the pyramid. In some of the very early pyramids, the mummy was buried in an underground chamber. In those cases, the pyramid itself was nothing more than a spectacular grave marker. But in the most famous of the pyramids, the mummy was housed in one of several chambers inside.

The passages leading to the burial chambers in the pyramids were sealed. The entrances may even have been hidden. So it seems quite reasonable to assume that there was some concern about tomb robbers. But if the pyramids were meant to discourage robbers, they were spectacular failures. For all the known pyramids of Egypt were robbed, not once, but many times.

The largest and most famous of all the pyramids, the Great Pyramid built for King Khufu, has stood open and empty for centuries. There is some evidence that after it was first robbed, it was used for later burials and resealed, then robbed again. The process may have been repeated several times. In the eighth century a Moslem ruler of Egypt could not find the entrance to the Great Pyramid, so he had his workmen cut a hole right through to the center. For centuries tourists have been climbing through the hot, airless passageways of the Great Pyramid to view the empty burial chamber.

Near the Great Pyramid is another pyramid called the Pyramid of Chephren. There was no obvious entrance to this pyramid, and many people thought that the monument was completely solid, with no burial chamber inside. Then, on March 2, 1818, Giovanni Belzoni, an Italian strongman who became the Egyptian agent for several European museums, smashed through the stones of the Pyramid of Chephren and

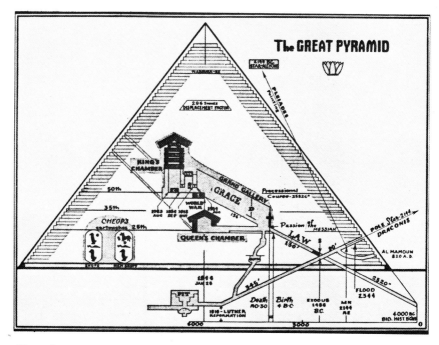

From time to time people have believed that the structure of the Great Pyramid contained all the secrets of the past and future. Here is a diagram of the interior of the Great Pyramid, which is supposed to show how various important movements in history can be traced. People who figure out such things call themselves pyramidologists; scientists call them pyramidiots.

located the corridor that led to the burial chamber. Since the tomb seemed completely sealed, Belzoni felt sure that he was going to find the burial chamber with all its riches untouched. He was wrong. The robbers had beaten him, probably by several thousand years. The burial chamber had been swept clean! Only the great stone vault that had once held the mummy itself was left, probably because it was too heavy to move.

A far more careful scientist was the Englishman Flinders Petrie. In 1889, Petrie found an unidentified and apparently unopened pyramid. Later he discovered he had hit upon the tomb of Amenemhet III, a major king of Egypt.

Petrie couldn't locate the entrance to the tomb. So he decided to cut a tunnel right through the masonry to the burial chamber. Since Petrie's funds and technical equipment were limited, this proved to be a terrible task. It took weeks of work under the broiling Egyptian sun. The work was not only hot, but extremely dangerous. At any moment the tunnel cut through the crumbling masonry might have collapsed, burying anyone who was there.

Finally, when the burial chamber was reached, Petrie discovered that the hole that had been cut was too small for him. Unable to wait until it was widened, he lowered an Egyptian boy with a candle into the vault. And by the flickering light the boy saw that someone had already been there. The chamber was empty.

This was a crushing disappointment for the archaeologist. But he began to wonder how the robbers had done it. After a great deal of trouble, Petrie finally did locate the cleverly concealed entrance to the pyramid.

Even after the robbers had found the entrance, they would have had to solve a variety of ingenious puzzles built into the pyramid to discourage robbery. Corridors were filled with stone blocks, passageways led to blank walls, and rooms were built without doors.

But somehow the robbers had managed to get through it all. Perhaps their secret was sheer brute strength, persistence, and good luck. But such a task would have taken months or years, and the robbers would have had to carry out their work in secrecy.

In the ancient days the pyramids were not just big tombs standing in the middle of an empty desert. They were religious monuments, regularly visited by pilgrims who wanted to pay their respects to the last earthly remains of the god-kings. The pyramids were also supposed to be tended by priests who performed the elaborate religious ceremonies needed for the kings' continued happy existence in the afterlife. Archaeologists have found documents that show that the kings set aside funds to provide for generations of priests to tend their tombs. At important tombs there would have been guards as well.

It seems that these priests and guards would surely have been able to detect the activities of the tomb robbers. But what if the priests and guards were actually in league with the thieves? Perhaps the very builders of the tomb provided the robbers with information on how to get around the blocked passageways and false doors.

Ultimately, Petrie decided that this is probably what happened at the pyramid of Amenemhet III. And some sort of cooperation between corrupt officials and tomb robbers must have resulted in the plundering of most of the royal tombs of Egypt. Some ancient Egyptian records hint at this.

Sometimes a robbery took place before the mummy was even buried. This may have been the case at the tomb of King Sekhem-khet. The king's burial vault was discovered in 1954 by Zakaria Goneim, a young Egyptian archaeologist. Though the tomb itself was in ruins, the stone sarcophagus (coffin) that held the mummy was undamaged and ap-

An early nineteenth-century drawing of the Great Pyramid, the Great Sphynx, and a sarcophagus from the pyramid.

parently untouched. The stone panel on the sarcophagus was sealed with plaster. It looked as if it had never been opened.

As Goneim watched the workmen struggle to lift the heavy panel, visions of King Tut's tomb danced in his head. It took nearly two hours for six men to raise the panel.

"I went down on to my knees and looked inside," wrote Goneim. "The sarcophagus was empty."

The same sort of story had been repeated hundreds of times in the history of Egyptian archaeology. And many tomb robbers, too, found that they had wasted their efforts on a tomb that had already been robbed.

Certainly both corrupt priests and the robbers themselves knew that they were violating not only a tomb but the tomb of a god. But they were not the only people in history to betray their religion for gold, and there was plenty of gold to be had in the royal tombs.

Didn't the "mummy's curse" frighten the robbers? It probably wouldn't have, even if there had been such a thing. But there wasn't. The so-called mummy's curse is a fraud.

Millions of words have been written about the fate of those who defied the curse and opened this or that tomb. The curse has been the basis of countless tales of terror. The idea of a mummy's curse became popular with the discovery of Tutankhamun's tomb, although the rumors of curses had been around for quite a while before that. After all, tombs are creepy places, and one gets the feeling that they should be cursed.

What really gave the King Tut curse tale a boost was the death of Lord Carnarvon, the man who had financed the discovery of the tomb. Carnarvon died suddenly and unexpectedly in Egypt just a few weeks after he helped open the tomb. Several other people connected with the discovery of King Tut's tomb also died within the next year or so.

Promoters of the curse legend play down the fact that Howard Carter, the man who really found the tomb and thus the man who should have been the primary target of any curse, lived on for many years, dying at a respectable old age. There were hundreds of people who were, in one way or another, connected with the discovery of the tomb. A few died shortly after the tomb was opened, and a few lived to be very old. Indeed, some were still alive at the time of this writing. That is just about what one would expect from any group in the population.

The cursed tomb and the mummy that rises from its coffin are standard features of horror films. Here in a scene from "The Mummy's Tomb" the evil priest, played by Turhan Bey, animates the mummy, played by Lon Chaney Jr.

There simply was no curse. There have been all sorts of rumors about a curse written over the door to the tomb or on some stone tablet found inside. The curse was supposed to have warned that death would come on "swift wings" to anyone who violated the tomb of the king. But there never was such an inscription in the tomb of King Tut. No one seems to know where or how the story started.

Many ancient peoples did place curses on their tombs; but the Egyptians, despite their fears of tomb robbers, did not. Nevertheless, the story of the mummy's curse has been repeated so many times that it has taken on a life of its own. No matter how often it is denied, there are always those who will choose to believe that there was a curse on Tutankhamun's tomb and that the curse was responsible for the death of Lord Carnarvon and many others.

It makes a good tale.

3

The Great
Tomb Robbery

It should have been obvious after a few hundred years that when it came to protecting mummies, pyramids were a flop. Pyramids got smaller and less showy as time went on, but that probably had more to do with the cost of the monuments than with any attempt to protect the mummies.

For nearly three thousand years the kings and other important Egyptians were buried in pyramids or other large and obvious tombs. And these tombs were always robbed. The tombs acted as magnets for the robbers. Building a pyramid was like putting up a sign reading: TREASURE INSIDE—COME AND GET IT.

The Egyptians were not stupid, but they were very conservative. They disliked any kind of change, and change came very, very slowly, if at all. But surely after a thousand or so years of tomb robbery, you might think they would have realized that their system just wasn't working.

It wasn't sheer conservatism that kept the Egyptians

from changing their burial customs, though. Religion also played a large part in the decision. Remember, the tomb of the king, or the tomb of any other important dead person for that matter, was a religious monument as well as a tomb. There were ceremonies that had to be performed regularly to insure the continued happiness of the dead man in the after-life. It was believed that these ceremonies had to be performed in a temple located very close to the spot where the mummy was resting. While you might be able to hide a tomb, you can't hide a temple where people constantly go in and out.

Around the year 1515 B.C. a major change in the con-struction of royal tombs finally took place. King Thutmosis I decided to have his tomb built in one place and his mor-

Interiors of two Egyptian tombs cut out of rock.

tuary temple in another. That may not sound very significant to you, but Thutmosis undoubtedly considered the change a big risk. Perhaps the ceremonies performed at a distant temple would no longer be effective and the king's *ka* would disappear, plunging him into eternal oblivion. But Thutmosis had to weigh this risk against the absolute certainty that within a very few years after his death his tomb would be plundered and his sacred remains violated and probably destroyed. Thutmosis decided to take the chance.

Separating the mortuary temple from the actual tomb meant that the highly visible temple could be built in one place where it would be easy to reach and the tomb could be hidden in a distant and remote spot. The place chosen for the tomb was an extremely desolate valley outside of Thebes, then the capital city of Egypt. The tomb was carved right into the rock of the valley cliff. The choice of this valley proved to be a popular one, for more than sixty of the kings of Egypt who succeeded Thutmosis I were buried there. The place has come to be known as the Valley of the Kings. It is a popular tourist attraction in Egypt today.

The innovation worked for a while. But ultimately the tomb robbers proved to be more clever than the tomb builders, and all the tombs in the Valley of the Kings were robbed—with the notable exception of Tutankhamun's tomb.

But for a while, the Valley of the Kings looked like a safe haven from the robbers. Thutmosis's chief architect, Ineni, bragged about the tomb he had built for his master and how closely guarded the secret burial place was. "I alone supervised the construction of His Majesty's cliff tomb. No one saw it, no one heard of it." That boast was found written on the wall of the architect's own tomb, which, incidentally, had been robbed.

Obviously Ineni didn't do all of the digging by himself. A large crew of workmen, perhaps several hundred, must have been used for the project, which probably took several years. Cutting Thutmosis's tomb into the cliff of the Valley of the Kings was not as complicated as building the Great Pyramid, but it was no small undertaking either. Perhaps the workmen were sworn to secrecy. More probably they were all killed after they had served their purpose. The Egyptians were not a particularly bloodthirsty people, however. There is no evidence that they practiced widespread human sacrifice or that they delighted in killing their enemies. But we do know that many other peoples have killed workmen in order to conceal the location of a tomb or a treasure. There is no reason to believe that the Egyptians would not have done the same.

Still, it is hard to imagine how even the most ruthless of kings would have been able to kill enough people to keep such a large project entirely secret. And he probably didn't, for Thutmosis's tomb was plundered, perhaps not too long after it had been built.

We have already mentioned that corrupt priests and guards were accomplices in many tomb robberies, but we cannot condemn them all. In fact, there seems to have been a fair number of priests and others who tried very hard to save the remains of their dead god-kings. Some scholars have speculated that there may have been a semi-official "cult of the dead," whose job it was to save the kings' remains from destruction.

This led to a curious phenomenon—the so-called wandering mummies. When a royal tomb was broken into, loyal priests would often remove the mummy (if it had not already been destroyed) to a safer place. Usually the safer place was some other royal tomb that had not yet attracted the attention of robbers. Royal mummies often had to be moved several times, and eventually large numbers of them accumulated in just a few tombs. The priests carefully listed a mummy's movements on its linen wrappings. The priests probably feared the effects of all this movement on the sensitive *ka*, but anything was better than having a mummy pounded to dust by robbers.

What a remarkable and weird scene it must have been.

The mummy transfers would most likely have taken place at night, to afford as much protection as possible from the tomb robbers' spies. Only a few of the most trusted would be involved in the transfer. Were they officials operating with the approval of the government, or were they religious zealots trying to save what to them were the most sacred objects in the land? Were there special prayers to be said when the royal mummy was moved, or was everything carried out in silence? We shall never know the answers to these and many other questions. All we know is that the mummies were moved from tomb to tomb within the Valley of the Kings.

Ultimately, the valley itself became too dangerous a place. Some forty royal mummies, including several of the greatest of the Egyptian kings, were gathered from various tombs, taken out of the valley, and hidden in a special mass grave in the desert, near a place called Deir el-Bahri.

Compared with the magnificence in which the kings had expected to spend eternity, the mass grave at Deir el-Bahri was a pretty bleak spot. It was a large, undecorated cavern that could be entered only by a narrow 35-foot shaft. The entrance to the shaft was carefully hidden. There were no golden statues or magnificent tomb furnishings in the underground cavern. But barren or not, this mass grave did the job. It protected the mummies from the tomb robbers for over two thousand years.

Then in 1875 the mass grave was found—but not by archaeologists. The archaeologists hadn't the slightest notion that such a grave existed. The grave was found by accident, and by tomb robbers. But what robbers! The accidental discovery of the mass grave was made by the leader of the Abd-

Mummy of Ramses II found in the mass tomb at Deir el-Bahri.

Ramses II as played by Yul Brynner in the film "The Ten Commandments."

el-Rasul family. The family had been in the tomb-robbing business since the thirteenth century. It was a profession handed down from father to son. But this mass grave was far and away the greatest discovery the family had ever made.

The mummies themselves were of little value, but a small number of objects had accompanied the kings to the mass grave. These were mere trinkets when compared to the magnificent furnishings that adorned the original tombs of each of these kings. But as far as the Abd-el-Rasul family was concerned, these trinkets were of enormous value. They would fetch an excellent price on the thriving antiquities black market that operated in the cities of Cairo and Luxor. The sales would have to be made with great care, however, to avoid attracting the attention of the government.

By 1875 the control of all artifacts discovered in Egypt was supposed to be entirely in the hands of the Egyptian government. Archaeologists needed special permission to work in the Valley of the Kings or anywhere else in Egypt. All finds had to be reported, and nothing could be sold or taken out of the country without government approval. Those were the laws. But the laws were not always obeyed. There were plenty of private collectors who were willing to pay huge sums of money for Egyptian antiquities, no questions asked. Even otherwise respectable museums were quite willing to buy objects that they knew, or had good reason to suspect, had been stolen by tomb robbers. The result was a thriving black market in Egyptian antiquities.

In those days the back streets of cities like Cairo and Luxor were filled with furtive men or small shops that offered stolen goods to likely-looking customers. The Egyptian government was trying to crack down on this activity, but it wasn't easy. There were too many robbers, too many eager buyers, and too few trustworthy policemen.

Although the government couldn't end the black market, officials were able to get a pretty good idea of the kind of stolen goods being offered for sale. In the early 1880s some rather unusual ancient objects began appearing on the black market. They were small statues and jars bearing the symbol, or cartouche, of some Egyptian kings. They were objects that had come from royal tombs. But the tombs of these kings had been discovered long ago—empty. The sudden appearance of the objects indicated that somewhere robbers had made an unusual and probably very valuable discovery.

The government's Department of Antiquities sent one of its own agents out to pose as a wealthy European buyer. The agent went to a part of Luxor known to be frequented by black-market dealers. He pretended to be a man who would pay top price for anything of real value. Finally the agent was able to locate the source of the objects, Abd-el-Rasul.

Abd-el-Rasul was promptly arrested and brought to trial. But at the trial he produced a stream of witnesses from his home village of Kurna. They claimed he was a good and honest man and swore that he had nothing to do with tomb robbing. This sort of testimony was hardly surprising. Through centuries of successful tomb robbing, Abd-el-Rasul's family had become one of the wealthiest and most respected in the entire village. Indeed, practically all the villagers were involved in tomb robbing in one way or another. But since no solid evidence could be produced against him, Abd-el-Rasul was freed.

Ramses II (far left) shown as one of the gods presenting gifts to a later king.

Everyone knew he was guilty, including the governor of the region. This particular governor had the reputation of being an unusually cruel man. He had the authority to hand out savage punishments to anyone convicted of tomb robbing. The members of Abd-el-Rasul's family were aware of this. They knew that the governor would be watching them, waiting for someone to make the slightest mistake. It would only be a matter of time until one of them was caught and convicted.

Finally, after a family dispute, one of Abd-el-Rasul's relatives went to the governor and confessed. Abd-el-Rasul himself was now squarely on the spot, so he agreed to give the government a valuable bit of information. In exchange, the government promised not to punish him for tomb robbing.

The information was so valuable that not only was the robber not punished, but he was rewarded. Abd-el-Rasul was given a job with the government department in charge of protecting ancient Egyptian archaeological sites from robbers like himself.

Abd-el-Rasul's information concerned the mass tomb at Deir el-Bahri. He had stumbled upon it quite by accident in 1875. It was unlike anything he had ever seen or imagined. The robber chief revealed the find only to the most trusted members of his own family.

Abd-el-Rasul was no fool. He knew that if a large number of objects from the mass tomb suddenly appeared on the black market, the authorities would become suspicious immediately. So he decided to leave the tomb intact, and take out just a few objects at a time for sale. Even this careful method of disposing of the find failed to go undetected by the authorities and led to his downfall.

On July 5, 1881, Abd-el-Rasul took a young man who worked for the Egyptian government to his find. The young man's name was Emil Brugsch. The entrance to the mass tomb was nothing more than a small hole in the ground. A rope was lowered into the hole. Brugsch carefully made his way, hand over hand, down the narrow 35-foot shaft. At the bottom he lighted his torch. He almost bumped into a gigantic stone sarcophagus. It turned out to belong to Seti I, an extremely important king and one whose empty tomb had been discovered some years earlier.

Carefully, Brugsch made his way among the profusion of coffins and mummies that were scattered about the large underground chamber. Whether the confusion and disorder were the result of the haste of the original reburial or had been created by robbers was impossible to determine.

Clearly, the royal mummies had long ago been stripped of much of their gold finery. But a great deal still remained, most notably the mummies themselves. When Brugsch finally totaled up the find, he realized that the chamber contained the mummies of forty kings, among them Thutmosis III, Egypt's greatest conqueror, and Ramses II, believed by many to have been the king of Egypt during the time of Moses. It was a moment of discovery not matched until Howard Carter's opening of the tomb of Tutankhamun.

Brugsch now had a problem. Since the location of the mass tomb was no longer a secret, other robbers would be quickly attracted to the spot. There was no way of effectively guarding the tomb from the attack of a determined robber band. So Brugsch decided to have the whole tomb cleared as quickly as possible and to send its contents on a steamer up the Nile to Luxor.

But who would do the job? The only workmen available in the area came from the village of Kurna, Abd-el-Rasul's home, where tomb robbing was a way of life. Could such men be trusted? Brugsch decided to take a chance. The following morning he hired about three hundred workmen. They certainly knew what they were doing, and they had a lot of previous experience getting things out of tombs quickly. Within forty-eight hours the entire contents of the mass tomb had been taken out of the underground chamber and were marked and ready for shipment. This had all been accomplished with such amazing speed that there was a delay of several days before the steamer arrived.

Word that the steamer was carrying the mummies of forty dead kings spread through the villages along the Nile. Hundreds of people rushed down to the banks to see the steamer, and crowds followed the boat as it passed. The men fired rifle shots in the air while the women threw dust on their faces and heads. Everyone was crying and groaning very loudly. It was the same scene that would have taken place at any large Egyptian funeral. Were the people showing respect for the dead god-kings of their ancestors? Or were they mourning the loss of a potential source of income? Brugsch, who watched the emotional demonstration from the deck of the steamer, was not sure, but he was deeply impressed by the sight.

4

The Mummy Trade

I can't walk through an exhibit of Egyptian mummies without getting a distinctly creepy feeling. When I was growing up in Chicago, I would occasionally visit the Oriental Institute, a museum that is part of the University of Chicago. The museum had a fine display of mummies, but not many people ever went there. A couple of times I found myself absolutely alone in a room full of dried and wrapped corpses. When I looked around and found that I was indeed alone, except for the dead things in the cases, I could feel panic rise inside me. As hard as I tried to control myself, I was unable to stay in that room for more than a minute. I would always flee to the comparative safety of the Assyrian exhibit or, if I was really scared, right out of the museum. Yet I would always go back to test my courage. And I would always fail.

I think that most people have this mixture of fascination and terror about mummies.

The professional tomb robber had to be less squeamish.

In fact, it appears that most tomb robbers did not find mummies particularly frightening or particularly interesting.

The whole point of the elaborate Egyptian burial ritual was to preserve the corpse of the dead person and provide it with the sort of goods that would insure a happy existence in the afterlife. The robbers were after the goods. The mummies themselves would not bring a high price. But mummies were often broken up or otherwise destroyed by thieves looking for jewelry that may have been hidden beneath the hundreds of yards of bandages. The robbers didn't have the time or the inclination to unwrap a mummy. They would just cut through the wrapping. The shattered remains of mummies were often found scattered about plundered tombs.

The mummified arm of an Egyptian queen was found hidden in a hole in her plundered tomb. The robber had evidently intended to pick it up later to get a jeweled bracelet off its wrist, but for some reason he was prevented from completing his robbery. Centuries later the arm with the bracelet still on it was found in its hiding place.

Practically every Egyptian except slaves and the very poor seems to have desired, and been able to afford, at least some degree of mummification. The Egyptians also mummified a large number of animals—cats, dogs, monkeys, birds, cows, even crocodiles. Many of these animals were sacred in the religion of the Egyptians, and making animal mummies was therefore a religious act. It is possible, however, that some Egyptians simply wished to have a favorite pet preserved so that pet and master could meet again in the next life. The Egyptians were known to be particularly fond of cats. They went into full-scale mourning when a well-loved household

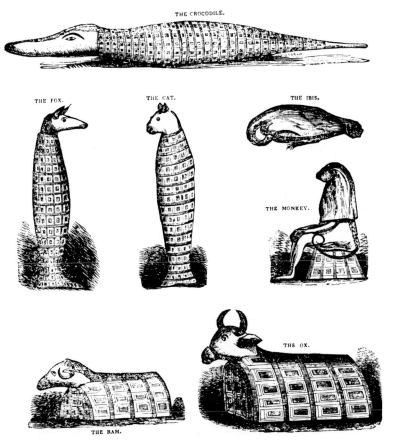

The ancient Egyptians made mummies from many different animals.

cat died. People who were strangers in Egypt and didn't know the customs might find themselves on trial for murder if they killed a cat, even by accident.

The practice of mummifying people and animals went on for thousands of years. As a result, Egypt contained a huge number of mummies. A hundred and fifty years ago Egyptian peasants used the wrapping stripped from mummies for fuel. When Europeans first became interested in ancient Egypt they paid little attention to mummies, which were far too numerous to be considered valuable.

Giovanni Belzoni, mentioned back in Chapter Two, was the circus-strongman-turned-purchase-agent for the British Museum and other European institutions. In reality, he was little more than a tomb robber with a respectable cover. But he wasn't really much worse than other late-eighteenth- and early-nineteenth-century explorers and exploiters of Egypt. He was just bigger and more flamboyant. Belzoni wasn't afraid of mummies. Indeed, he often found himself nearly up to his neck in them. Describing his entrance into a mass tomb, he wrote:

> It was chocked with mummies. I could not pass without putting my face in contact with some decayed Egyptians. But my own weight helped me on. However, I could not avoid being covered with bones, legs, and arms, and heads rolling from above.

The mummies, which were usually thoroughly dried out and quite fragile, might actually present a danger. One risked being smothered by mummy dust, as Belzoni noted:

> In such a situation I found myself several times, and often returned exhausted and fainting . . . . Though fortunately, I am destitute of the sense of smelling, I could taste that the mummies were rather pleasant to swallow. After the exertion of entering such a place, through a passage of fifty, a hundred, three hundred, or perhaps six hundred yards, nearly overcome, I sought a resting place, found one, and contrived to sit. But when my weight bore on the body of an Egyptian,

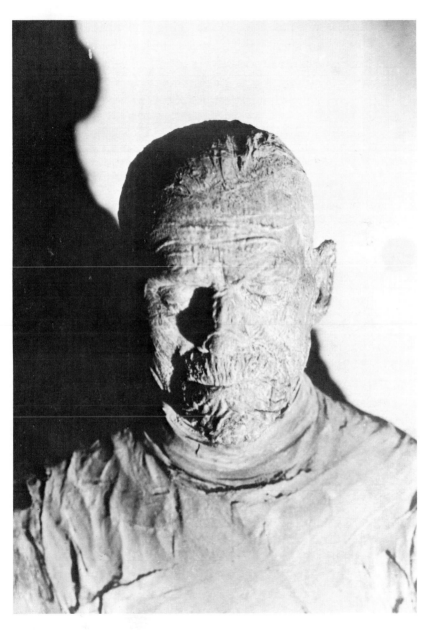

Boris Karloff as the original Hollywood mummy from the film "The Mummy."

it crushed like a band-box. I naturally had recourse to my hands to sustain my weight, but they found no better support. So that I sank altogether among the broken mummies, with a crash of bones, rags, and wooden cases, which raised such a dust as kept me motionless for a quarter of an hour, waiting till it subsided. I could not remove from the place, however, without increasing it and every step I took I crushed a mummy.

Belzoni was no respecter of the dead.

Then, in a curious and rather roundabout way, some European physicians decided that mummies were good for you—that ground-up mummies made good medicine. Suddenly the mummies themselves, not just the treasures in their tombs, became valuable. This opened up new opportunities for tomb robbers.

Since medieval times, physicians had prescribed powdered bitumen, a black, glasslike substance, as a cure for a variety of ailments. Actually, bitumen didn't cure anything, but then most medieval medical treatments were useless if not actually harmful. At least bitumen didn't make the disease worse.

Bitumen's chief value was that it was expensive and hard to get. People figured that anything costing so much must be good for something. They also swallowed gold dust, powdered "unicorn horns," and "dragon's teeth" as medicine.

The best bitumen came from Persia, where it was called *mum*. When Europeans began exploring the tombs of Egypt, they somehow got the idea that the preserved bodies of the ancient Egyptians had been soaked in liquid bitumen and that that was why they were so well preserved. In fact, various

Christopher Lee played the mummy in several British mummy films.

other substances, mostly resins, were poured over the linen wrappings. These hardened into a black material that resembled bitumen. Arabs began calling the wrapped bodies themselves *mumiyah,* which became *mumia* in Latin, and finally *mummy* in English. And that is how the mummy got its name. *Mummy* is not an ancient Egyptian word.

Anyway, this "bitumen" from the mummies began to appear in Europe, where physicians immediately declared it superior to the substance from Persia. Why, people wondered, was bitumen so good at curing diseases? Some people made the apparently logical assumption that the curative powers came not from the black substance soaked out of the mummy's bandages but from the preserved body itself. Therefore, why not use the pulverized corpse as medicine?

43

Mummies, like other movie monsters, always seem to carry off the heroine in a nightgown.

That seemed a very good idea. Besides, the whole mummy produced far more powder than could be obtained by soaking hundreds of yards of linen bandages to get a small supply of resin. But even as the supply of mummy powder increased, so did the demand. The Egyptian government began to fear that the country would run out of mummies, so it clamped down hard on the activities of the tomb robbers.

Tomb robbers, however, proved to be infinitely resourceful. When their supply of old mummies was blocked, they began producing instant mummies. The process is simple enough in hot, dry Egypt. The modern mummy-makers purchased the corpses of people who had died in prison or who could not afford a proper burial. If this supply was not sufficient, they might resort to robbing recent graves.

All the insides were removed from the corpses. Then they were soaked in a cheap blackish material called asphaltum. The bodies were then wrapped and allowed to dry in the sun for a few weeks. The result was something that looked very much like a thousand-year-old mummy.

European physicians began to lose their faith in the curative powers of powdered mummy. They also feared that these instant mummies might be made from corpses of people who had died of infectious diseases, and that the disease could be transmitted. Gradually, physicians stopped recommending the substance to their patients. But by then mummy powder was so popular that many people went on using it anyway. Eventually, the supply of mummies ran out and this particular cure disappeared from the European scene. What had happened was that the Egyptian government, which was always strapped for funds, kept raising the taxes on the "mummy factories." Finally they were taxed right out of the mummy-making business.

Clearly, tomb robbers and collectors like Belzoni had little respect for, or fear of, mummies. But over the last century or so the mummy itself has developed the most eerie and sinister reputation. Most people whose knowledge of Egyptian burial customs comes primarily from films and television, have the general impression that the tombs were supposed to be protected by the mummies themselves. They seem to think that the mummy's curse was a magical operation in which the mummy got up out of its sarcophagus and strangled or otherwise disposed of all intruders. As we have already noted, the ancient Egyptians did not place curses on their tombs. The walking mummy idea is sheer nonsense. It has no basis whatever, either in fact or in ancient folklore. Such an idea is the invention of writers and movie-makers.

Yet a whole stream of movies with titles like *The Mummy, The Mummy's Curse, The Mummy's Tomb, Revenge of the Mummy,* and so forth, has implanted the walking mummy image deeply into our consciousness. The mummy of the movies is a murderous monster, staggering about, dragging yards and yards of dirty linen bandages. The mummy, along with Dracula, Frankenstein's monster, and the Wolf Man, has become one of filmdom's scariest creatures.

Of course, if the ancient Egyptians had wanted their mummies to walk around, they wouldn't have wrapped their legs together or bound their arms across their chest. Before a mummy could move, it would have to be able to unwrap itself. Otherwise, it could do nothing but roll about helplessly on the floor. How was a mummy supposed to get out of the stone sarcophagus in which it was placed? But there is no point in trying to bring reason into such a discussion. The mummy should be enjoyed as a creature of horror fiction.

Guards who work in the Egyptian collections of museums say that they are regularly approached by people who will swear that they saw one of the mummies in the collection move. No amount of reassurance will change their minds. I must say that when I was alone in the mummy room of the Oriental Institute, I was sure the mummies would move, though they never did.

I have only run across one case in which a museum

The mummies of the Incas were often wrapped in a bundle.

mummy actually did move, and this mummy happened to come from Peru, not Egypt. The case was recounted by Egyptologist John A. Wilson:

> The story goes that the Field Museum [in Chicago] many years ago received a shipment of mummies from Peru. They had been crammed down into barrels, tightly flexed inside the wooden containers. The foreman of the basement workers said, "Jim, knock the head off one of those barrels. Let's see what's in them." Jim went to work and loosened the head of a barrel. He had just succeeded in getting it free all the way around, when the head of the barrel flew off, a mummy rose up before him, making a whooshing noise as the air rushed into its body. With the release of the pressure, the body resumed its outstretched position. Jim left suddenly, without discovering what the shipment was.

5

The Fate of
The Robbers

It was obviously murder. Bloodstains were still plainly visible on the wound and on the victim's dress. Even a quick examination showed that the girl's throat had been cut. Robbery couldn't have been the motive, for nearby lay a leather satchel crammed with jewelry and other valuable objects. And alongside the body was a bundle of brightly colored cloth also containing jewelry.

There wasn't much point in calling the police, however, because the girl had been dead for about fifteen hundred years. The body was discovered in the twentieth century; the murder had been committed in the sixth century.

The body was discovered in the 1930s at a place called Qustol in Nubia, south of Egypt. An expedition headed by Walter B. Emery was excavating burial mounds. The mounds had been built by people who were known as the X-group, simply because no one had ever come up with a better name for them. The X-group people were closely associated with

48

Egypt, but they rose to power late in Egyptian history—long after Egypt had become a province of the Roman Empire. Still, both the art and burial customs of the X-group were heavily influenced by traditions stretching back to the days of the pyramid builders.

While digging through one of the large burial mounds, Emery came upon what, he said:

> at first appeared to be a bundle of gaily colored cloth, but as we cleared away the sand and rubble, we were faced with a very gruesome discovery; the bundle of cloth was the linen garment of a young girl who had obviously been murdered. The body was naturally preserved, a phenomenon not uncommon in Nubia when the remains have been buried in dry sand and rubble. The girl's body was so little decayed that it was plain to see how she had met her death . . . .

So Emery and his associates knew how the girl had been killed, and they began to speculate about the motive for the murder. They had been digging in the burial mounds of Qustol for some time and knew that the X-group people had been enthusiastic practitioners of human sacrifice. Large numbers of servants and others had been killed and buried in the tomb along with a dead king.

But this death did not seem to be part of the regular sacrifice ritual. The body had not been placed in the burial chamber or any other special place. It had just been tossed on top of the mound and hastily covered with sand and gravel.

Here was a fifteen-hundred-year-old murder mystery. Emery could not resist making some guesses as to what might have happened. The first possibility that came to mind was that the girl had been meant as a sacrificial victim but had escaped from the general sacrifice, only to be run down and killed by guards.

But if she had been running for her life, it hardly seems likely that she would have burdened herself with a heavy satchel and a bundle, no matter how valuable their contents. She would not be able to use the jewels after she was dead.

The two parcels of jewels and a nearby empty chest with a broken lock all suggested robbery. Perhaps the girl was a tomb robber who was caught by guards and executed on the spot. But why didn't the guards then return the jewelry and the chest to the tomb from which it had been stolen? Or, at the very least, why didn't they steal it themselves after killing the real thief?

Pushing speculation just a little bit further, Emery suggested that the murdered girl was one of a group of thieves. For some reason they had a falling out, and they killed the girl because they feared she knew too much. But the presence of the two jewel-filled parcels makes this suggestion difficult to support as well. Would the thieves, who had risked their lives in the first place, leave behind such treasures? That hardly seems likely.

After that, Emery ran out of suggestions. He commented, "Anyway, here we have a murder mystery of fifteen hundred years ago and there we must leave it."

So far, we have concentrated on the profits of tomb robbing, but there were risks as well, as the girl at Qustol may have found out.

There was always the danger of being caught, of course. If one was in league with guards or local officials, that risk

Working inside a tomb could be a difficult and dangerous task.

must have been reduced considerably, but still it was a risk. An honest official might ruin the whole scheme.

Then there was the danger of going into a tomb at all. The passages were narrow, the air was foul, and at any moment there might be a cave-in that would entomb the robbers as well as the dead they were trying to rob.

Archaeologists who regularly work in ancient tombs are well aware of these dangers and take whatever precautions they can. Even so, lives have been lost and many famous archaeologists have told harrowing tales of narrow escapes from collapsing walls or ceilings. The tomb robbers rarely had the luxury of slow and cautious work. They had to do the job in a hurry, often at night. They would hardly have had the time to build supports and props for crumbling ceilings. The job simply had to be a dangerous one.

Archaeologists have found the body of more than one unlucky robber inside the tomb he was trying to rob. In 1970 archaeologists found the skeleton of a robber in a tomb being excavated near the pyramids at Giza. The man had been crushed by a limestone block that had fallen from the ceiling. From the position of the skeleton, the archaeologists figured out that he was trying to reach inside a sarcophagus when the block fell and killed him.

Now, since tomb robbery in the Giza area was probably more common in ancient times than modern (because Giza is a well-known place and usually well watched), it was assumed at first that these were the remains of an ancient robber. But closer examination showed that a rotted garment draped around the skeleton was a suspiciously modern-looking coat. The case was clinched when a Cairo newspaper was found inside the coat pocket. The date on the paper was still faintly legible—1944!

Probably the most striking bit of evidence about the consequences of tomb robbing comes from the ancient Egyptians themselves. The Egyptians were fanatic record-keepers. Most of their records were written on a paperlike substance called papyrus. Despite the Egyptian climate, which is very good for preserving materials like papyrus, the vast majority of ancient Egyptian records have been lost over the centuries. Nevertheless, a surprisingly large number has survived. In fact, there are thousands of rolls of Egyptian papyrus in museums all over the world that remain unread simply because there are not enough scholars to do the job.

Among the records that did survive is an astonishing document from the Twenty-first Dynasty and the reign of Ramses IX (1144–1123 B.C.). The document describes, in detail, the trial of a group of tomb robbers and shows how the robber bands operated in ancient times.

The Twenty-first Dynasty was a bad time for Egypt but a good time for tomb robbers. The ancient kingdom on the Nile was tottering toward its final extinction as an independent state. The plundering of tombs reached new heights (or depths). The robbery involved not only corrupt priests and guards, the corruption reached high up into the government.

The document tells of Peser, the mayor of Eastern Thebes and the good guy in the story, and Pewero, mayor of Western Thebes and the bad guy. It seems that robbers had been systematically stripping the burial grounds on the western side of the Nile. It was Pewero's job to protect the tombs in his region, and he wasn't doing it. In fact, he was profiting from the robbery. Peser found out about this and denounced Pewero to the governor of the entire district, a man named Khamwese. Khamwese set up a committee to investigate the charges.

The committee was stacked against the honest Peser. The document hints that Khamwese himself might have been involved in the payoff. When the committee issued its report, it dismissed Peser's charges on technicalities. Peser said that ten royal tombs had been robbed; the committee said only one. Peser said that the tombs of four priestesses had been rifled; the committee could find only two of the tombs that had been broken into, and so on. The committee ignored the obvi-

In films, the mummy rises up to kill any intruders. In fact, no one in ancient Egypt ever seriously thought that the mummy would rise up to protect its own tomb.

ous issue—that there had been a great deal of tomb robbery in Western Thebes. Pewero got off scot-free.

The document goes on to describe how Pewero struck back at his enemy. He got all the guards and workmen from the burial areas, men who doubtless participated in the robberies, to cross over the river and demonstrate in front of Peser's home. The demonstration was too much for Peser. He swore that he was going to bring the case directly to the king.

According to the ancient record, that was an error—a bad one. As I have already mentioned, the ancient Egyptians were very conservative. They wanted everything to be done the way it had been done before. If you thought something was wrong, you were supposed to report to your immediate superior. You were not supposed to try to go over his head. Going directly to the king was certainly going over Kham-

wese's head. That was not only a mistake but a crime. Peser was found guilty of this crime.

But there is a happy ending to the story. The document reveals that just two or three years later, Peser's charges were proved correct when a band of tomb robbers was caught and (after some painful persuasion) confessed.

The robbers gave a detailed account of how they opened the coffins and found the king's mummy:

> There was a string of amulets and ornaments of gold at its throat; its head had a mask of gold upon it; the mummy of this King was overlaid with gold throughout. . . . We stripped off the gold which we found on the mummy of this god. . . . We found the King's wife likewise; we stripped off all that we found on her. . . . We set fire to their coverings. We stole their furniture, which we found with them. . . .

The names of five of the eight robbers captured have come down to us: Hapi, the stonecutter; Iramen, the artisan; Amenemheb, the peasant; Kemwese, the water carrier; and Thenefer, the slave. They were all executed for their crimes. Whether the high officials who helped the tomb robbers ever suffered for their involvement in the crimes is unknown.

In any case, it is safe to assume that most tomb robbers got away cleanly and went unpunished. Trials like the one described in this document were fairly rare, and they didn't discourage other robbers one bit.

6

Tomb Robbery in Italy

Egypt is not the only land that has been plagued by tomb robbers. Any country with a long history has also had some people eager to make a quick buck out of that history. Italy has a longer and richer history than most countries. For that reason, it has had more than its share of tomb robbers. And no region of Italy has suffered more at the hands of tomb robbers than Tuscany. Tuscany was once the home of a rather mysterious people called the Etruscans.

The Romans, unlike the Egyptians, did not favor elaborate burials. They cremated their dead and placed the ashes in simple tombs. The Etruscans, however, were very different. They sent their departed off into the next world accompanied by a host of worldly goods. Thus, they became perfect targets for the tomb robbers' art.

Let's back up for a moment and find out just who the Etruscans were. During the fifth and sixth centuries B.C. they were the most powerful people in Italy. The base of their power was in a group of city-states in the central Italian region known as Tuscany, which is a modern corruption of the word *Etruscan.*

The Etruscans were the chief early rivals to the rising power of Rome. But unlike the Romans, who were superb organizers, the Etruscans never could get together. The Romans defeated their cities one by one. By about 200 B.C., Etruscan power was broken forever. The Etruscans didn't abruptly disappear. They were simply absorbed into the general Italian population over the next few hundred years. Some of the leading Roman families boasted Etruscan ancestors. But slowly most knowledge of Etruscan history, language, and customs was lost and, the Etruscans came to be regarded as a mysterious people.

The Etruscans were not native to Italy. They came from somewhere else, probably in the East, but no one is sure where. Their language was unlike that of any other known people. We have a few tomb inscriptions in the Etruscan language. But if they produced any poetry or literature, it is now gone. Etruscan cities have, for the most part, disappeared.

All we have left are the Etruscan tombs. Fortunately, Etruscans lavished a lot of attention on their tombs, and they can tell us a great deal. For the tomb of a wealthy man, the Etruscans dug out a large underground cavern, which was then outfitted like a house. A poor man's tomb was simply a smaller, cheaper version. The Egyptian tomb was also considered a "house of the dead." This had led many to conclude that the Etruscans were somehow influenced by the Egyptians.

The Etruscans made no elaborate attempts at mummifi-

Tomb built for a favorite of Alexander the Great.

Tomb of Prince Mausolus of Caria, designed by Greek artists. It was considered one of the seven wonders of the ancient world.

cation. That would have been useless anyway in Italy's damp climate. The body was placed in a stone sarcophagus, with a likeness of the dead person carved on the lid. These figures are probably the most remarkable pieces of funeral art to be found anywhere at any time in history. The Egyptians usually represented the dead person in some grim pose. But not so the Etruscans. They were more likely to show the dead person reclining on a couch, his head propped up on one elbow. It is a very lifelike and good-humored pose. Frequently the person is shown with a slight smile on his lips. This smile is so common in Etruscan art, and yet so unlike anything found in other art, that it has been called the Etruscan Smile.

Etruscan tombs were filled with jewelry, statues, pottery, and a host of other objects that the dead people might need in the next world. The walls of large Etruscan tombs were covered with paintings of Etruscan life. The scenes are usually joyful ones of hunting, banqueting, and sports. But sometimes darker and more violent scenes can be found in the tomb paintings. The Etruscans did practice human sacrifice, and some paintings have led authorities to believe that the Etruscan view of the afterlife may have been a rather horrifying one. But we can't be sure. Without any written information, it is hard to guess just what the Etruscans believed.

The Etruscans were known as excellent craftsmen. Their gold work was especially fine. Much of this gold was buried in tombs, but practically none of it has survived into modern times. Virtually all important Etruscan tombs were plundered centuries ago. The gold was stolen and melted down.

The objects from one of the rare unplundered Etruscan tombs fill an entire hall of the Vatican museum. One can only guess at the treasures that have been lost over the centuries.

The early tomb robbers were most interested in the obvious valuables like gold and jewelry. More humble objects were often broken or just left where they had been found. The entrances to the underground tombs were sealed up or simply became overgrown. Over the centuries, the vast Etruscan cemeteries came to resemble ordinary fields dotted with small hills. The original location of most Etruscan tombs was forgotten, as farmers planted crops over them.

Then in the early nineteenth century, people began to rediscover the Etruscans. It would be more accurate to say that Etruscan art, or anything else connected with the Etruscans, became popular once again. People willingly paid large sums of money for anything Etruscan. This booming market in Etruscan objects gave new life to the tomb robbers of Tuscany.

Tombs that had been robbed already were robbed all over again. This new generation of tomb robbers was not looking for gold and jewels, although the thieves would certainly pounce happily on any that they found. The new tomb robbers were looking for pottery, small statues, and any other humble objects that had been overlooked by their treasure-hunting predecessors. These simple objects would bring high prices.

Legally, all Italian antiquities that are discovered belong to the state. The government will pay a fee for every object found, but this fee is tiny when compared to the object's worth on the black market. As a result, tomb robbing in Italy has proved almost impossible to stop.

The robbers themselves are usually poor farmers who are not getting rich on what they find. They sell what they steal to a middleman for a modest price. The object may be resold several times, eventually for quite a bit of money. But the original robber only gets a small portion of the final sale price. Still, considering that the income from farming the region is low, it is a welcome source of additional funds.

Undisturbed Etruscan tombs can look like small hills.

Local police generally know who is robbing the tombs. But, unless the robbers are caught in the act of actually breaking into a tomb, it is difficult to convict them. Even if they are convicted, the punishment is rarely anything more than a small fine. The tomb robbers consider such fines just part of the cost of doing business. And often the robbers can get away scot-free by offering the police a small bribe. The police are not highly paid either, and many need the money.

A basic problem is that most people in the region just don't think there is anything wrong with tomb robbing. They don't see why the money from the finds should go to the government rather than to the poor farmers who really need it. They resent archaeologists, who are outsiders, coming in, digging up their land, and carrying away objects that they believe should be theirs.

In many ways the tomb robbers have a point. But even though we can sympathize with their position, that does not make it right. As far as archaeology is concerned, the tomb robbers are terribly, terribly wrong.

One of the reasons the Etruscans seem so mysterious to us today is that there has been so much tomb robbing. A carefully excavated tomb can tell us a great deal more than a group of objects of unknown origin on sale in a dealer's shop. Tomb robbers are also careless. They break many objects or toss them away as useless. Tomb paintings, which cannot be removed, have often been destroyed by robbers.

Unfortunately, tomb robbing will go on as long as there are plenty of buyers for illegal Etruscan antiquities. In fact, the buyers who have the money are really more to blame than the robbers, who are poor men.

But when it comes to buying black market Etruscan antiquities, let the buyer beware. For the manufacture of phony Etruscan antiquities is a far bigger business than the robbing of Etruscan tombs. It has been estimated that anywhere from 70 to 90 percent of the Etruscan artifacts sold on the black market today are modern fakes.

These objects are not sold as reproductions. Manufacturing reproductions of antiquities is a perfectly honorable business. But these fakes are sold as the real thing for much higher prices than reproductions would bring. The casual tourist can be easily fooled by fakes. Only an expert can tell the difference between a good fake and the real thing. And even the experts are fooled sometimes, probably more often than they would like to admit.

Etruscan fakes were responsible for the greatest embarrassment in the history of New York's prestigious Metropolitan Museum of Art. In 1915 and 1916 a purchasing agent for the Metropolitan bought three large "Etruscan" statues for the museum. One showed a rather elongated warrior with a white beard, another a stocky and rather oddly proportioned warrior. The third was an enormous head of a warrior. All three statues had been broken and had to be pieced together. They were the largest Etruscan clay statues anyone had ever seen.

Just how much the museum paid for these three works is unknown, but it was surely a substantial amount. The agent warned the museum to keep quiet about its new purchases because he had not yet had time to check the site of the excavations where the works had been found. The men he purchased the statues from he referred to as "rogues." They had

Likeness of an Etruscan couple carved on the lid of a sarcophagus. Note the "Etruscan smile."

reputations as tomb robbers and were being secretive and difficult. The agent kept trying to find out exactly where the statues had come from until 1924, when he lost touch with the rogues.

The museum finally got tired of sitting on its find. In 1933 a new gallery of Etruscan art was opened at the museum. The three large statues were the most spectacular part of the exhibit. They were an immediate hit with the public. But a few questions were raised in Italy and America. By 1937 there was a real battle going on among scholars. Some insisted that the statues were fakes. Others, equally qualified, were just as sure that the three pieces were genuine.

Another Etruscan sarcophagus lid. This time the statue is not smiling.

The battle went on, but by the late 1950s the case for the authenticity of the statues was beginning to crumble. The big break in the case came in 1958 when a retired art dealer named Harold Parsons found a man who claimed that he had actually helped make the statues. The man's name was Alfredo Fioravanti. He claimed to have made the statues along with Riccardo and Virgilio Riccardi, two men who had once worked in the pottery business.

From about 1900 to 1920 the three had made many forgeries. Most of their fakes were small pots. The three clay statues were the most ambitious projects they had ever attempted. In fact, one of the statues was a little too ambi-

The colossal head of an Etruscan warrior, which turned out to be a fake.

tious. The three forgers made the larger of their two warrior statues in a small rented room. When they got as far as the waist, they realized that the figure would be too tall to fit in the room. So they simply squashed down the upper part of its body. That is why the statue looked so oddly proportioned.

By 1958 the Riccardis were dead and Fioravanti had been out of the forgery business for years. He had been telling stories of how he and his associates had faked the statues for a long time. But was he to be believed? Perhaps he was just bragging to attract attention.

Fioravanti said he had proof. After the statues were made they were broken up. This was partly to make them look old, for few ancient clay statues survive in one piece. Also, because the clay had to be baked to harden and the forgers did not have a very big oven, they were forced to bake the statues in pieces.

Fioravanti had kept part of the statue of the big warrior as a souvenir. It was the thumb of the left hand. The statue in the Metropolitan was missing its left thumb. Fioravanti produced the thumb, and when it was placed on the left hand of the museum statue, it fit perfectly. There was no longer any doubt.

The embarrassed museum withdrew the statues from public exhibition, and they are now stored in the museum basement. Many other Etruscan works of art on display in museums have turned out to be fake as well, and still more are seriously suspected.

Where tomb robbing is common, the opportunity for forgery is great.

7

They Escaped

By about this time you may be getting the impression that every ancient tomb in the world has been opened long ago, and thoroughly plundered. But that is too gloomy a conclusion. It is possible, more than possible, that Tutankhamun-like discoveries will still be made in the future. After all, before 1922 very few people thought that the nearly unplundered tomb of an Egyptian king would ever be found.

There are a number of famous tombs that have not yet been found. There is reason to hope that at least some of them were missed by the tomb robbers as well.

Probably the most thoroughly lost tomb is that of the great thirteenth-century Mongol conqueror, Genghis Khan. Genghis Khan started as the head of a small tribe of impoverished horsemen. In fact, at one time his enemies reduced his power to a mere handful of followers and he was on the run for his life. But by the time he died, his warriors had conquered much of China to the East and had made forays into

Europe in the West. They owned everything in between. No army in the world could stand against them. Genghis Khan's sons enlarged the Mongol conquests, making the Mongol Empire the largest the world has ever known.

Genghis Khan was an absolutely ruthless conqueror. His wars resulted in the death of millions and the enslavement of millions more. Therefore, he is often depicted as some sort of monster—but he was more than that. He was a military and political genius, perhaps the greatest the world has ever known. No one has ever started with so little and wound up with so much.

Genghis Khan died on August 24, 1227, and no one knows where he is buried. He was an old man by that time, but he was leading his horsemen on one last conquest. His death occurred far from his native Mongolia. It was vital for the Great Khan's successors to keep his death a secret as long as possible. News of his death would undoubtedly set off rebellions all over the newly won empire. The Khan's sons were scattered all over the empire. They needed time to come together and consolidate their power.

So as Genghis Khan's funeral procession made its way slowly back to Mongolia, anyone who had the misfortune to observe it was instantly killed by Mongol soldiers.

Before Genghis Khan, the Mongols did not have elaborate burials. They were too poor. The Great Khan could have provided himself with a funeral of unparalleled luxury. But if he did, we don't know anything about it. Neither the Great Khan's personal tastes, which were simple, nor Mongol tradition would lead us to believe that he was buried in a magnificent tomb. However, it is doubtful that his followers would

We have no drawings of Genghis Khan that were made when he was alive. This is a Chinese artist's idea of how he was supposed to look.

This is how Genghis Khan looked in the movies.

have thrown his remains in an unmarked hole in the ground either.

There are two legends regarding the conqueror's burial place. One holds that he was buried in secret somewhere on Mount Kentey, the sacred mountain of the Mongols. The other says that his body was never buried, but was kept as sort of a sacred relic by some of his successors. Much later, when the Mongol Empire was breaking up, some of the competing rulers said that they possessed the real remains of Genghis Khan and were thus the true heirs to his power. But this second legend does not date back to the time of the Great Khan's death. It also sounds suspiciously like a self-serving political myth.

The secret burial on Mount Kentey is probably closer to the truth. It is possible that even today someone knows where the tomb is but just isn't telling. Genghis Khan was, and to a certain extent still is, worshipped by the Mongols. Obviously, back in the thirteenth century, someone, probably a fair number of people, had to know where he was buried. That knowledge may have been handed down from generation to generation as part of a secret tradition. While the Mongol Empire is long gone, the direct descendants of Genghis Khan still live in Mongolia.

In any event, there will probably not be much searching for the grave in the immediate future. The reason is political. Mongolia is now completely under the influence of the Soviet Union. Genghis Khan is not one of the Russians' favorite historical characters, since the Mongols conquered and ruled Russia for a long time. In fact, Genghis Khan is one of the real villains of Russian history. Genghis Khan is also regarded as a symbol of Mongolian independence. Independence is not the sort of thing the Soviets wish to encourage. They even discourage celebrations marking the birthday of Genghis Khan. It seems that even after eight hundred years, Genghis Khan is capable of stirring up emotions.

Someday, however, the tomb of this world conqueror may yet be discovered. And no one knows what it may hold.

There is some controversy about the tomb of another world conqueror, Alexander the Great. Alexander was the Macedonian king who in a short span of about ten years conquered much of the known world. He died in 323 B.C. at the age of thirty-three. His final illness struck him in Babylon while he was returning home from his conquests.

Alexander the Great as played by Richard Burton in a film biography of the con-queror. The woman is Claire Bloom.

It is well known that Alexander's carefully preserved remains were seized by Ptolemy, one of Alexander's generals, and taken off to Egypt. Ptolemy was to become ruler of Egypt. He thought that the physical possession of the great man's remains would add prestige to his position. He put the carefully embalmed corpse in a magnificent tomb in the city of Alexandria. There it became a shrine. For centuries people all over the world came to visit the tomb of Alexander.

Then, as Egypt fell into chaos, Alexander's tomb simply disappeared. It is believed to have been destroyed during riots that swept the city in the seventh or eighth century. But no one really knows. Some archaeologists suspect that, at the very least, some remains of the tomb can be found in Alexandria. But today Alexandria is a thriving city. You can't dig up an entire city just to look for a tomb, no matter how important.

Recently, however, some archaeologists have come to believe that they have found the tomb of Alexander's father, Philip, king of Macedon. He was a great conqueror in his own right, although his deeds have been overshadowed by those of his more famous son.

A fairly large, and apparently royal tomb has been located in Macedonia. It is unplundered. Though it does not contain the sort of riches brought out of the tomb of Tutankhamun, it is certainly a remarkable find. But is it Philip's tomb? Unfortunately, there are no names anywhere in the tomb. The tomb's discoverers believe that it is. Other archaeologists are not so sure. Everyone agrees, however, that it is a great and important find.

Then there is what may turn out to be the greatest archaeological find of modern times, one that may ultimately outshine even the discovery of the tomb of Tutankhamun. It is the tomb of the Emperor Ch'in Shih Huang Ti. Now admittedly the name Ch'in Shih Huang Ti is not exactly a household word in the West. But then neither was Tutankhamun until 1922. The major difference is that while Tutankhamun himself was historically insignificant, Ch'in Shih Huang Ti was enormously important in Chinese history. In many respects he was really the founder of China.

The future emperor started out as the king of the small state Ch'in. At the time, the land was divided up among a number of small states, all constantly warring with one another. Ch'in was one of the smallest and weakest. Yet the king of Ch'in managed to overcome all his rivals, and in the year 221 B.C. he proclaimed himself emperor of the land that we now know as China. From that date until the revolution of 1912, China was always ruled by an emperor. The name China itself comes from the name Ch'in.

Shih Huang Ti ruled his empire with ferocious efficiency. He had the Great Wall of China built to keep out the northern barbarians. The Great Wall, which stretches some fifteen hundred miles, is a building project that rivals and perhaps surpasses the Great Pyramid. The Great Wall took thirty years to build and cost the lives of countless thousands of laborers. Today the Great Wall remains China's number one tourist attraction.

As he grew older, Shih Huang Ti became obsessed with the prospect of his own death. He had survived several assassination attempts and was terrified of another. He traveled constantly between his 270 different palaces, so that no one could ever be sure where he was going to be. He never slept in the same room for two nights in a row. Anyone who revealed the emperor's whereabouts was put to death along with his entire family.

Shih Huang Ti searched constantly for the secret of immortality. He became prey to a host of phony magicians and other fakers who promised much but could deliver nothing.

The emperor heard that there were immortals living on some far-off island, so he sent a huge fleet to find them. The commander of the fleet knew that if he failed in his mission, the emperor would put him to death. So the fleet simply never returned. It is said that the fleet found the island of Japan and stayed there to become the ancestors of the modern Japanese.

In his desire to stay alive, Shih Huang Ti did not neglect the probability that he would die some day. He began construction of an immense tomb in the Black Horse hills near one of his favorite summer palaces. The tomb's construction took as long as the construction of the Great Wall—thirty years.

The emperor, of course, did die. Death came while he was visiting the eastern provinces. But his life had become so secretive that only a few high officials were aware of his death. They contrived to keep it a secret until they could consolidate their own power. The imperial procession headed back for the capital. Unfortunately, it was midsummer and the emperor's body began to rot and stink. So one of the plotters arranged to have a cart of fish follow the immense imperial chariot to hide the odor of the decomposing corpse. Finally, news of the emperor's death was made public. The body, or what was left of it, was buried in the tomb that he had been building for so long.

Stories about that tomb sound absolutely incredible. It was said to contain miniature reproductions of all the emperor's 270 palaces. A map of the entire empire with all the major rivers reproduced in mercury, which by some mechanical means was made to flow into a miniature ocean, was also part of the interior of the tomb. So was a reproduction of the stars and planets. According to legend, the burial chamber itself was filled with molten copper so that the emperor's remains were sealed inside a gigantic ingot.

A section of Shih Huang Ti's Great Wall.

It was also said that loaded crossbows were set up all around the inside of the tomb, and that anyone who did manage to penetrate the inner chambers would be shot full of arrows. But just to make sure that no one got that far, the pallbearers who had placed Shih Huang Ti's remains in the tomb were sealed inside with it. They were supposed to be the only ones who knew exactly how to get in and out of the intricate tomb. All of this was done to preserve the emperor's remains from the hands of tomb robbers. Did it work? We don't really know yet.

There are two contradictory stories about the tomb of Chi'in Shih Huang Ti. The first says that it was covered up with earth to make it resemble an ordinary hill and that its location has remained unknown for centuries.

But a more accurate legend holds that there never was any attempt to disguise the existence of the tomb. Ch'in Shih Huang Ti had been building it for years, and everybody knew where it was. After his death the tomb was surrounded by walls enclosing an area of about five hundred acres. This was to be the emperor's "spirit city." Inside the spirit city were temples and all sorts of other sacred buildings and objects dedicated to the dead emperor.

Over the centuries the walls, the temples, indeed everything above ground was carried away by vandals. The top of the tomb was covered with earth and eventually came to resemble a large hill. Locally the hill is called Mount Li. But still the farmers who lived in the area had heard stories that Mount Li contained the tomb of Ch'in Shih Huang Ti or of some other important person.

Could this fairly obvious tomb have escaped the clutches of tomb robbers?

One account relates that about four years after the emperor's death, his tomb was desecrated by an invading army. At the time of his death Ch'in Shih Huang Ti was not a popular man. He ruled chiefly by force. After his death his successors were not able to hold on to power. Revolts broke out in many parts of the land. Following a lengthy civil war a new group established itself on the throne of China.

During the civil war it is entirely possible that enemies of the old emperor tried to destroy his tomb.

But did they succeed, and if so, how much damage did they do? And what about more conventional tomb robbers? Imagine all the damage they could have done over the centuries. Archaeologists have generally assumed that even if they could find the tomb, it would be fairly empty. But a recent discovery has changed that opinion, and Chinese archaeologists are now very hopeful.

In the spring of 1974 a peasant plowing a field near Mount Li uncovered a life-sized clay statue of a warrior. Further digging indicated that there was an entire army of statues beneath the ground. Though excavations are not yet complete, Chinese authorities believe that there are some six thousand life-sized clay statues of warriors, plus scores of life-sized statues of horses. Most of the statues are broken, but some are in an absolutely remarkable state of preservation. Each statue is finely made, and each shows a distinct individual, different from all the others.

This incredible collection is Shih Huang Ti's "spirit

army." At one time Chinese kings practiced human sacrifice so that the victims could serve the dead king in the next world. Shih Huang Ti was willing to make do with models. Men and horses were arranged in a military fashion in a three-acre underground chamber. The chamber may have been entered at some point. The roof certainly collapsed. But still the delicate figures have survived surprisingly well. Most of the damage was done when the roof caved in. That is why the Chinese archaeologists are so hopeful that when the tomb itself is excavated, it too will be found to have survived surprisingly well.

The Chinese are not rushing the excavations. They have only a limited number of trained people to do the job. After all, the tomb has been there for over two thousand years. A few more years won't make much difference.

Though once denounced as a tyrant, Ch'in Shih Huang Ti is now regarded as a national hero. His name is a household word in China. The Chinese government knows that it may have an unparalleled ancient treasure on its hands, and it wants to do the job well. Over the next few years we should be hearing much more about this truly remarkable find.

Even Egypt, although it seems to have been thoroughly picked over by robbers for thousands of years, may yet hold a few surprises. Walter Emery, whose excavations of the tombs of the X-group people at Qustol in Nubia we discussed earlier, was looking for the tomb of Imhotep. Emery was digging at a place called Saqqara in Egypt. It is the site of the Step Pyramid, Egypt's first pyramid, indeed the first large freestanding stone structure ever built.

Imhotep was not a king. He was a government official,

an architect and many other things. He designed the Step Pyramid for King Zoser. In later ages Imhotep was considered a god, the patron god of wisdom. Imhotep was no god, of course, but he may very well have been the first genius that we know of.

He almost certainly would have been buried at Saqqara near the tomb of the king he served. It is known that Imhotep's tomb later became a shrine that was often visited by worshipers from many nations. But the exact location of the tomb was lost.

Emery spent a lot of time digging in the Saqqara region. He thought he had found evidence of the tomb, but he died before he could make any major discovery. The search, however, continues.

There is even hope, admittedly faint, that we may someday learn more about the famous heretic king Akhenaten, predecessor of Tutankhamun. Akhenaten's own tomb was found completely empty and badly mutilated. It seemed obvious that the king's enemies had vented their fury upon his tomb after his death. But there is no evidence that Akhenaten's mummy was ever placed in the tomb. In fact, it seemed that the tomb had not really been finished. If Akhenaten's mummy wasn't in the tomb, then where was it?

In 1907 Theodore Davis, a wealthy amateur archaeologist, discovered a tomb from Akhenaten's time. It contained a mummy in a fairly bad state of preservation. Davis thought he had found the mummy of Queen Tiye, Akhenaten's mother, for her picture, along with that of her son, was found painted on a wooden panel in the tomb. But closer examination later showed the mummy to be that of a man.

The only known contemporary likeness of the Emperor Ch'in Shih Huang Ti.

Some authorities immediately insisted that Akhenaten's mummy had been found in this rather humble tomb. But others said no, the mummy was of a man far too young to have been Akhenaten. It must be the remains of Smenkhkare, who may have reigned briefly between Akhenaten and Tutankhamun. A recent reexamination of the mummy indicates that it almost certainly is that of Smenkhkare. But no one knows what a royal mummy was doing in this rather simple tomb. The tomb that Davis found had already been pretty thoroughly plundered. Davis himself was only a well-meaning amateur. He did not record his find with scientific accuracy. If he had done so, we might know more.

And there is still another mystery. From time to time small objects like statues and vases that may have come from the tomb of Akhenaten appear on the black market in Egypt. This has led some to wonder if perhaps modern tomb robbers have located a "secret tomb" for the heretic king. Akhenaten surely realized that as soon as he was dead his enemies would try to destroy his final resting place. He must have had supporters who would have tried to protect his mummy. Perhaps they hid the mummy somewhere, only to have it found thousands of years later by tomb robbers. Although it may sound farfetched, it is still a possibility. That sort of thing has happened before.

So, as I said, even Egypt may yet hold some surprises. Although tomb robbers have been depressingly successful throughout history, they certainly have not plundered every tomb. If they had, you would probably never have heard of King Tutankhamun.

OTHER BOOKS WITH INFORMATION
ON TOMBS AND TOMB ROBBING

BRACKMAN, ARNOLD C. *The Search for the Gold of Tutankhamen.* New York: Pocket Books, 1977.

CERAM, C. W. *Gods, Graves and Scholars.* New York: Knopf, 1967.

————. *The March of Archeology.* New York: Knopf, 1958.

COHEN, DANIEL. *Ancient Monuments and How They Were Built.* New York: McGraw-Hill, 1971.

————. *Secrets From Ancient Graves.* New York: Dodd, Mead, 1968.

COTTRELL, LEONARD. *The Tiger of Ch'in.* New York: Holt, Rinehart and Winston, 1962.

CORMACK, MARIBELLE. *Imhotep, Builder in Stone.* New York: Watts, 1965.

DEMPEWOLFF, RICHARD (ed.). *Lost Cities and Forgotten Tribes.* New York: Pocket Books, 1976.

DESROCHES-NOBLECOURT, CHRISTIANE. *Tutankhamen.* New York: New York Graphic Society, 1963.

EDWARDS, I. E. S. *The Pyramids of Egypt.* Baltimore, Md.: Penguin, 1961.

EMERY, WALTER B. *Lost Land Emerging.* New York: Scribners, 1967.

HAMBLIN, DORA JANE. *Pots and Robbers.* New York: Simon and Schuster, 1970.

MCHARGUE, GEORGIS. *Mummies.* Philadelphia: Lippincott, 1972.

PACE, MILDRED MASTIN. *Wrapped for Eternity.* New York: McGraw-Hill, 1974.

RICHARDSON, EMELINE. *The Etruscans.* Chicago: University of Chicago Press, 1964.

INDEX

mummification, Egyptian, 11–13,
  23–24, 38–39
"mummy," etymology of, 42–43
"mummy's curse," 19–22, 45–46

Nefertiti, Queen, 7

Oriental Institute of the
  University of Chicago, 37

papyrus, 52
Parsons, Harold, 67
Peser, 53–56
Petrie, Flinders, 17–18
Pewero, 53–55
pharaoh, meaning of, 14
Philip, King of Macedon,
  possible tomb of, 76
Ptolemy, 75
Pyramid of Chephren, 15–16
pyramids, 13–19, 23, 82–83

Qustol, burial mounds of, 48–50,
  82

Ramses II, King, 4, 5, 35
Ramses IX, King, 53
Riccardi, Riccardo and Virgilio,
  67–69
Roman burial customs, 57

Sekhem-khet, King, 18–19
Seti I, King, 4, 34
Shih Huang Ti, see Ch'in Shih
  Huang Ti
Smenkhkare, 8, 85

spirit city of Ch'in Shih Huang
  Ti, 80, 81–82
Step Pyramid of King Zoser,
  82–83

Thebes, 25–26, 53–56
Thutmosis I, King, 4, 24–27
Thutmosis III, King, 35
Tiye, Queen, 83
tombs, Egyptian, 5–9, 13–36,
  40–42, 48–56
  hazards in, 51–52
  mortuary temple separated
    from, 24–27
  "mummy's curse" and, 19–22
  pyramids as, 13–19
  robbing of, 5, 15–23, 28–34, 38,
    40–42, 50–56
tombs, Etruscan, 58–64
  faked artifacts from, 65–69
  robbing of, 61–64
  sarcophagus in, 60–61
tombs, undiscovered:
  of Alexander the Great, 74–76
  of Genghis Khan, 70–74
Tutankhamun, King, 1–10, 12,
  20–22
  tomb of, 5–10, 12, 20–22
Twenty-first Dynasty (Egypt),
  53–56

Valley of the Kings, 7, 8, 25–28,
  31

Wilson, John A., 47

Zoser, King, 4, 83